LET'S PLAY!
LITTLE CHAMPS

SWIMMING

RYAN JAMES

NORWOOD HOUSE PRESS

Library of Congress Cataloging-in-Publication Data

Names: James, Ryan.
Title: Swimming / Ryan James.
Description: Buffalo, NY : Norwood House Press, 2025. | Series: Let's play! little champs | Includes glossary and index.
Identifiers: ISBN 9781684502325 (pbk.) | ISBN 9781684502332 (library bound) | ISBN 9781684502349 (ebook)
Subjects: LCSH: Swimming--Juvenile literature. | Aquatic sports--Juvenile literature.
Classification: LCC GV837.6 J359 2025 | DDC 797.2'1 --dc23

Published in 2025 by
Norwood House Press
2544 Clinton Street
Buffalo, NY 14224

Designer: Ocean Books
Editor: Kim Thompson

Photo credits: Cover, p. 1 Patrick Foto/Shutterstock.com; p 5 YanLev Alexey/Shutterstock.com; p. 6 Andrii Medvednikov/Shutterstock.com; pp. 7, 16, 17 wavebreakmedia/Shutterstock.com; pp. 8, 9 Krzyszstop Winnik/Shutterstock.com; p. 12 Suzanne Tucker/Shutterstock.com; p. 13 Shestakov Dmytro/Shutterstock.com; p. 14 Studio Peace/Shutterstock.com; p. 19 Marcos Castillo/Shutterstock.com

Printed in the United States of America

CPSIA compliance information: Batch #CW25NHP: For further information contact Norwood House Press at 1-800-237-9932.

TABLE OF CONTENTS

What Is the Sport of Swimming?

Swimming is a fun activity, and it is also a sport. Swim teams **compete** at swimming **meets**.

The Uniform

Tight, stretchy swimsuits help swimmers move easily in the water.

Goggles help swimmers see underwater. Swim caps keep hair out of the way.

5
4

The Pool

Swim teams use long pools with **lanes** that are marked by ropes. Each swimmer has a lane. Every lane has a **starting block** for swimmers to stand on before they dive in.

The Strokes

A stroke is a way to move your body through the water. For a freestyle stroke, you stretch one arm forward while the other arm pushes water behind you. You kick your legs up and down.

For a backstroke, you lie on your back. You **alternate** your arms in a windmill motion. Your legs kick up and down.

For a butterfly stroke, you move both arms together in a big circle above the water. You kick both legs together in a wavy motion, like a dolphin's tail.

For a breaststroke, you move your arms in front of you before pushing the water back. You kick your legs out and together like a frog.

Practice

Swimmers begin practice by warming up. This gets their muscles ready and keeps them from getting hurt.

Swimmers practice their strokes. They get stronger and more skilled. They try to make their motions smooth and fast.

Swimmers work on their starts and turns. These are important for quick changes during races.

Coaches time swimmers to **track** their progress. This helps swimmers know what they need to improve before a meet.

Relay Races

Some races at a meet are relays. Four swimmers each take a turn swimming one part of a race. When one finishes, the next one begins. They touch the pool wall to tell the next swimmer to go.

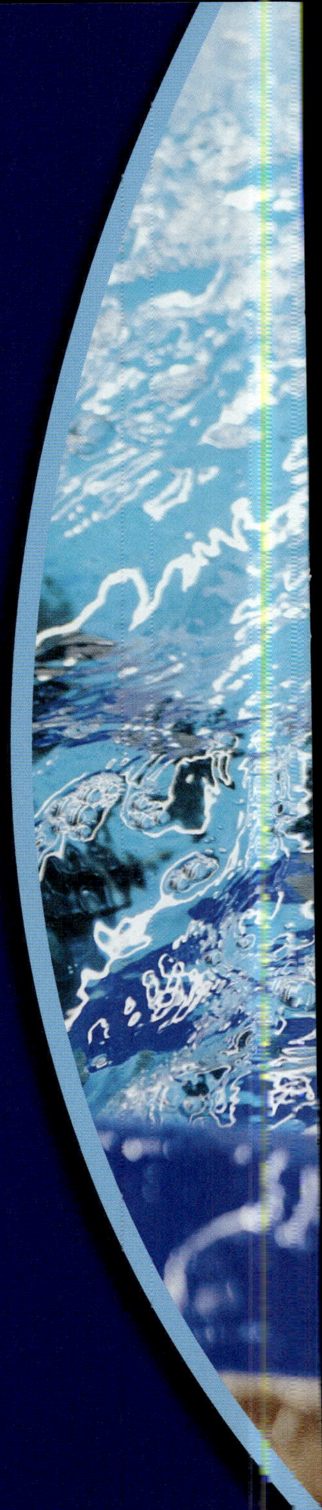

How to Be Meet-Ready

Swimmers should eat healthy foods like fruits, vegetables, and lean meats. They should drink plenty of water. Getting enough sleep gives them **energy** to swim their best.

GLOSSARY

alternate (AWL-tur-nate): to take turns; to go back and forth between two things

compete (kuhm-PEET): to try hard to do better than someone else in a game or competition

energy (EN-ur-jee): the ability to do work

goggles (GAH-guhlz): protective glasses that fit tightly around your eyes

lanes (lanes): parallel courses into which a swimming pool is divided

meets (meets): sports competitions between teams

starting block (STAHR-ting blok): a box or low platform at one end of a pool on which a swimmer stands before the start of a race

track (trak): to follow, make note of, or record; to keep track of

THINKING QUESTIONS

1. What do swimmers wear?

2. Why do you think the breaststroke might be easier than the butterfly stroke?

3. What do you think makes a relay race difficult to do?

4. Why do swimmers need to eat healthy foods?

5. What qualities do you think a good swimmer has?

INDEX

ABOUT THE AUTHOR

Ryan James lives in the western part of North Carolina with his rescue dog Bailey. As a child, he would search for creepy crawlies as he hiked through the forest near his house. When he's not on the hiking or biking trail, he is cheering on his favorite baseball and football teams.